BOILED OWLS

AZAD ASHIM SHARMA

BOILED OWLS

NIGHTBOAT BOOKS
NEW YORK

ISBN: 978-1-64362-235-4

DESIGN AND TYPESETTING BY KIT SCHLUTER
TYPESET IN PLANTIN MT PRO AND NEUE KABEL

CATALOGING-IN-PUBLICATION DATA IS AVAILABLE
FROM THE LIBRARY OF CONGRESS

NIGHTBOAT BOOKS
NEW YORK
WWW.NIGHTBOAT.ORG

CONTENTS

For Fellowship & Family

[A CUBIST PORTRAIT OF THE WRINGER]

Again I collect every last bit of the liver;
It's been a while since I held a feast for the eyelashes.

—MIRZA GHALIB,
tr. Frances W. Pritchett
and Owen T. A. Cornwall

Let me hear nothing of the moon, in my night
there is no moon, and if it happens that I speak of
the stars it is by mistake.

—SAMUEL BECKETT

At the nineties' afterparty's afterparty's afterparty: I tried writing a letter to tell you what I needed to justify my experience without someone else's voice but as I said I've got no image to return to 'cause so much depended on drugs and that's such an obvious thing to say it's obscure.

Everyone loves giving it about desire and affect; more time I try not to know too much, rezoned in a place where we can go fishing for cuttlefish. You know it's all the same to me. Sometimes, the talking fucks the therapy.

I was down in the DSM in a clinic, triaged myself—woke up with a new brain after every rotation; the drugs stopped working and I just need to take a moment. I stumbled into the psychoanalyst's office; he told me some of us aren't ready to let go of the security our parents lied about.

She found me covered in my own sick in the shower, checking my pulse into the recovery position; do you know how much sleep I've lost? I shout at the people I love and lie to them when I mean to tell them the owls have boiled.

I didn't want to work in finance to fund a broken habit. That much transparency I could give her. I met with the damned to learn how to be allergic to money & what I'm saying is I've been the day's patient. If they still worked I'd still be out there but now I'm surrounded by teeth, ordered on the shelves. I drank again last night. All I want is that old place back: to be malleable, to fall.

I forgot to change the water in yesterday's flowers.

Unwashed it pounds
      into breathalysed marrow   after a spree
loved ones   radical feminists
      are made into detectives   my pupils dilate
uplift wears itself into descent
      embeds with the force   of a concrete duvet
a stimulant can be a sedative   can be the tear
      my rib's discontinuous fan whirring its rattle
we turned home into *Zuchthäusern*
      I slept for the first week off the sauce

a pickled turnip staring at a spreadsheet
      of what I owed and to who —
I want to worry about how much I will consume
      at lunch or in the evening
these are real problems of subsistence
              they will be the death of...
how much money   do we need
      to be   to not give   mental space over
to what has to be paid and when?
      The worst thing I ever did was learn.

Came down off synthetic psychedelics   the streets
of Epsom,
       parks and recreation
              that was all I did
couldn't get served at seventeen
so impecunious
            dotted lemon haze & amnesia
silver papers
           ducked chequered uniforms
held it up every day
                a baton for freedom.
Then there were house parties
       middle class grammar school types
          looked at me with suspicion
ringing my phone on Fridays asking for a feeling   still—
I was high off it all
      the clout and the nous
         didn't get a charge or a fine
            but that's just chance.
College   the same deal
         the drugs turned angry or weird
had to nurse emotions
           I flirted with the sea
before I heard a blue note and still had white teeth in
hard boiled wonderlands
      a rave going nowhere
           heart doing the distance.
I could describe that love I felt for strangers
     with solid black walls of clammy ecstasy
doing an eighth of criticism

over someone's assignment

of second-hand furniture

lost a few to white heroin in the 'dam

in the end our ways go separate

it all got too much

& all I've got before the line comes

white bags,   plastic straws.

HIGH MODERNIST RELAPSE

I was impossible on the *Stultifera Navis*.

A ship's petrified bow beat me into reason.

I had come off the Renaissance's horizon.

Sublime melancholia parallaxed as a self.

I was in search of a line to change everything.

Iseult shouted where land ended on a crest wave
arched, fallen.

A shortened stem from the high grass came up
restless in the rushes.

Zero-point of Spring teased white-grey.

Twelve naked trees swayed with chance and
neurochemistry.

Amour, ennui: life's great spectacle
blighted by the absolute limit of exits.

Comminations in the genitive erupted
from the tall flowers.

Old choices sprung with frisson.

Glassed eyes chartered a path.

I—soul of spirit drunk to preserve
art's skiff of self-knowledge.

Lodged in ambiguity by the sail's catalepsy.

Passed through exclusion's fleshless threshold
and its bifurcation of perception.

This half-imaginary geography of all that came to be
as real as an orange.

You look to me and say
the fifteenth century was so unkind.

The clouds buried me with their tiny esoteric tears.

Caliban left shadow-spots on our moon, gibbous.

I could speak about the science but the truth is
I've lost my freedom.

On the ship of fools I met with a band of drunkards,
cokeheads, junkies.

Common to us is our absence of choice; our bodies fixed
to the fractured masts wreathed by fatigue.

Simple words had lost their magic and significance.

The last leaf in my body, shaken.

COMEDOWN MUZIK

Depression   clouds in   to my body.
I sit down   at the edge   of the world   on a stairwell

& fill your cup as mine empties—you know we could
keep drinking   until you've reached   your limits?

I am frustrated!   I'll have to find other friends
whose cups are empty   of vows to not carry on.

This is   the most authentic essay
about a great downturn   in my suburban life:

I wake up naked   on the patio   covered in rain.
There will be more cups   yes   I'll fetch them right now,

I'll do it all again   with friends or alone,   & magic
mutinous cantos about minerals, rocks,   soiled linen.

The mind is a wrong place   someday I'll come back
O—   the odds on survival vary too much.

VENLAFAXINE

You say isn't it strange that you're still addicted, taking this pill
every day? Because you're so empathic to the pain in the world.
The sharp razor of your hindsight blunted, oceanic. I pined for
a way out of the low reef. If I don't take pills a deep sadness
crawls out I know more of limits, you know my bandwidth is a
little narrow, affects don't rise the way they do in other people,
and my feelings are indecent, vapid. I let you in on it: I did so
much cocaine to not feel in that sedation I was embodied just
for a moment; then it was around my throat, a band of longing I
prayed for moths, bees, snowdrop, aconite, redwood and in this
open way as the fates stitch me together I agreed with you: it is
strange. Every night I hovered over dust convinced it was the
right drug. I stared at a rocky outcrop, my mind a sequence of
echoes I try to justify being porous to this Warm Wide World. I
tell you I'd like new experiences of high-definition paintings or
a lucid, happy memory I need you to know how much I need or
think I need is killing me, stealing our slow time together, shut-
ting us away from feint pulses of daylight. You make the case for
selflessness, tolerance, fortitude in humility and I'm hearing you
with eyes closed; yesterday I forgot to breathe in the meeting
failure turns an ethics out of learning and I share this with you
over my eighth cup of coffee explaining how an addict doesn't
know how to love because I didn't know how to forgive myself
and stop carrying this —

EVERY NIGHT WAS FULL OF
FORGETFUL ENCOUNTERS

so I said a prolonged farewell   to alcohol
inside a   conch on the shores   of personhood

I addressed   the fantasist
he doesn't see   optimism's cruelty;

I whisper to   the pythoness   by a bronze age stream
drinking   opoponax impercipient   to gravity

its insistent apostrophe   towards slow death.

In a letter   I wrote   *one day at a time*
there's always a bleed   tomorrow   or the day after

I ask the ink   who really knows   what's coming
around that bend   on the horizon?

Kept   a moment on   the limited   emotional quotient
I allow   myself to write   with.

The letter   apprehends   purpose,
stimuli,   their chaotic   seizure

of every spare thought I made room for—   I want
a wild life in letters   all those peaks made a flat line.

[RITUALS FOR IRRITABLE PERSONAE]

Wrenched from the matrix, that is where oblivion
begins to suppurate, no, deracinated memory, the
being uprooted from its lives, the white sea day
after day impossible but still there.

—ÉDOUARD GLISSANT,
tr. Nathanaël

TIME MANAGEMENT

I am a hot lobster
    canned inside your all-day breakfast
        life has never felt more tedious

my lungs full of wishes, tar, carcinogens—
    shall we have another coffee together
        or have we drunk enough industrial food?

What goes on in the world escapes me
    the window is unappealing, too reflective,
        its glare pushes me to a sentimental mood.

Influencers appear in the wild grass
    desiccated acorns feigned to psychology
        they explain the value of time management;

how urgent productivity really is:
    I could add so many more days
        to this day were I more awake, present.

It's not that I am unconnected
    more that I can't cope with adult talk
        of meaning in a post-internet apocalypse.

EVERYDAY LIFE POEM
After Rimbaud and Hélio Oiticica

Here, pain is a rich tapestry of historical subjectification
& more lines will flow as dysregulated animal sensoria

lo!   in moonlit atmospheres the vortices have me
sovereign, synchronic, somnambulant, mortality checked

by the good life running course as I clutch this new day.
My forehead a salt-lake enclosure distorted to obliquity

in glass stained green   with hindsight's bitter pill.
Geopolitics tints   tradition's wayside   grunge

and I am raging at the point of narcocapital's promise:
parcellated happiness in grainy levamisole's rotted flesh.

Borderline with my atoms I try to help other people find
the lettuce   my functionality   still masks the contours

I took your palm close to me and rubbed out my eyes
focused on yr unconscious constellation: a public feeling.

TAKING A WALK

What can I do when I encounter another person

except to yearn for all of our lost connections?

I felt nothing for a decade—only extremities

or a semiotics premised on exchanging value

all around the roads gladdened by nostalgic ire.

I slept all through the day smudged in a blur,

walked with you a little longer to the Capital

where fascism grows as silent as a stillborn.

Under canopies of sleet I paused for air

took public subsidy to try and work it out

held back in a centre for dismal recreation

with abrupt shifts in the lexical geography

tripping over my own toes turned cicatriz

in burnt sienna, health: my selfless priority

made me present for the people I love

or willing to not hate those I loathe.

This art that I tried to make out of illness

down the shutter goes to capture that moment.

I wrote it down and threw it to the breeze

held a world in an inhalation for a whole minute

my nerves a grapefruit in scordatura

crows would caw to my loud hands

read by a gnarled oak's demure welcome.

Tawwaf I go calling out to infinite rehearsal

& this body I'm in given over to the exegete

my diagnoses like signals on my forehead.

At life's great proscenium I amble home

in the ordinary weather with this rough going

a twisted logic, a mute compulsion, a decision

I'll renounce when my face isn't so swollen.

XENOBIA

I ask you how you've slept
                          better than before
you dragged me through matter's rash expenditure,
appealing to
                          the Qur'an's cuneiform raga
time once again music
                          singular,
      the effect
we're grounded in
                          sweat & musky,
                                    the notions—

I'm no longer an I.P.A.

You held me
            lazy at the low end of beautiful
                  and desire peeled over estimation.
It will reproduce itself
            as necessity,
            irrespective of how I smell just after the rain.

I implode into difference   outwards   a world

with logic under my arm I was put on notice

until midnight.
                              I'm thinking again of you
giving me a choice I was so late to act upon
                  your cadence falling on my forehead

The best mother I could've wished for as an atom.

HER POEM

A new attitude that won't kiss
    damage to our constitutions.

I cheated on you with a substance
    that difficult hymn.

You are tired of hearing apologies
    this amends is living

in my abdomen
    tense with the past's sun.

After patience wears down to heal
    with pearled relation

there is forgiveness
    in our romantic comedy

away in a silent song your smile
    a big screen.

In the morning I fall in love
    with you again   you are again

I wake up to your moonflower face
    held slow for two green hummingbirds.

SINUS RINSE CONVALESCENCE

I laid down on liquid modernity's vertical axis
to saline rinse flaked remnants out of my cheeks
an overdose a day's more than I'd bargained for

horripilation in sepia celluloids I couldn't stand
up it went on for years & years. The consultants
placed my using career in a list of consequences

would've made more sense if I'd been punched
in the face *but that was five years ago* I replied.
I wolf down antibiotics to prevent perforation

of my deviant, jelly-like septum that smells just
as chlorinated as the steroid burns like the drip
before I can breathe through both nostrils & sigh.

PLANETARY DEATH IS A
HOPELESS DRUG ADDICT

Self-appointed judiciaries of counterculture
complain the twelve steps I take are cultish
& I should blame total administered society.

Well I'm not so sure but I know loving our
selves militantly from not-being grotesque,
misanthropic with self-sabotage. We found

that fourth dimension insightful to disavow
capital, its benthos. I pick up more resentments
from the unregulated newsreels.

I can communicate today and deep the pain
without a blind code, scabrous or rusticated.
You need to know how much I resent the world

for its beauty is right at my throat burning
away my tobacco skin. I am decayed in floods
held perishable by extraction's funk in the seas

as nuclear excrement defenestrates coevals
of contrarian data, all those staccatos of denial.
I reach out as worldliness ready to throw away

my dissolute self-turned hurricane to disaster's
manhandled future opened on the returned past.
I'm sick of fighting currents, toxic with our need

of currency & hope for revolution. It is too late
to be stuck at a party putting apathy to rights
or knelt at your altar praying for an easy day.

> O this scene of death.
> The clouds are full of lightning,
> we are the wired.

TOOK ME THIRTY YEARS
TO SAY THE FOLLOWING

I'm not okay and when did this mediocre and trite mood come to represent something aspirational or desirable? I do not think saffron will cure me of these sad boy aesthetics. In the open materiality of things I am estranged from symbol, sign, and self, made into air that was universal exchange, a sentence lived right up to executions. I am interminable; at an impasse with relief's enclosure of complexity, fraught and turning on the chromatic hinge that white is substantial and I become property as its consumer. I'm so insincere with objects that used to hold the passage of time, but this sort of séance doesn't shift the need for care in the midst of whatever we mean by constraint. History breaks into lines and back on its own inheritance of oblivion. Again resentment offended me for an entire year; my aura was bilious green and overstimulated. I was having the same argument with myself; the repetition drove everyone else mad or worse — away. I was lost in the scroll to attention seeking and attention giving; addicted to digitality and its pastiche of life on the street where broken glass gifts me science fictions, organic blueberries, labour power, resilience.

I thought of my grandparents' spirits they had navigated so much uncertainty to get me back to give this testimony disfigured by a lost freedom. I can't remember the sound of their laughter.

Serious eyes appear pixelated by heavy air the intervention begins with my cousin Tariq. He cannot live this life without me at his side. When Aunty Coco told me she was so proud—you could have died—my stomach expanded by the parade

& a local addict approached yelling *seahorse!*

Papa waited until my birthday I smell his arms as if for the first time we begin to have a conversation. I make amends to my brother & he grabs my face *you're getting better* he said it twice *you're getting better.*

The clearest communication between us.

My lover and I watch movies together laughing after a good day's work after a good night's rest. My mother now asks for advice never failing to remind that she told me to meditate first. People ask me what my higher power is—

I know what I'm thinking about when I'm thinking about Love.

BIRTHDAY SONG

You know about surrealism too
  watching Thomas the Tank Engine
    as I read Fred Moten's *Stolen Life*
      on Sesame Street I tried to hide
        my breakfast lines from you
      and made art from yearning.
    Unlike typical siblings
  we fought in a red silence
grainy with domestic neorealism
  I want to be someone for you
    present in this life and after
      holding your face as you held mine
        no longer in fear of tomorrow.
      This morning you asked me
    if it was fine that you took
  my slippers worried
I think my feet would be cold
  on the slate tiles in our kitchen.
    It will be fine. You said it
      twice. It will be fine.
        The slate is cold
          I don't mind
        it wasn't cold in the sun.
      We saw another slate tile
    in a carriage from North Wales,
  but it was in Amberley,
an ornament in a working museum.
  I'm unsure why I want
    to historicise a space
      where no-one will historicise.

I love you without regard
for your astrological chart.
I love you because you are.
You wanted to know
if it'll be fine if you could
take my slippers this morning.
It will be fine today is your day,
I thought I would write it down.
On the way she explains
traffic signs, from the back
seat we don't drive we track
ourselves on a digital map,
on the simulacrum: a concept
I don't think I can explain
to you or to myself,
I am curious. The city
is the greatest con-artist;
she acknowledges the true
thief of living conditions
there is more space here.
Echolalic thereafter, you
make sounds that escape
they tell me you are excited.
There was Bank Cottage;
turning to a hidden entrance.
She explains diagonal black
what those lines mean
all clear you can go sixty
but only real country folk do.
Cousin Tariq is devilishly asleep,
you address him
by his mother's name.
Auntie Coco you say, pointing.

We explain lineage;
you say Auntie Tariq.
    Two carers lead the way
        Your other carer is at home
            fixing the jasmine lattice
                on the front yard.
                    We are all sad.
                A sadness tinged.

SRI AUROBINDO SAYS ADDICTS
ARE YOUNG HEGELIANS

In the nether world I passed you with clogged pores transformed
in quaint anticipation of unruffled peace.

Brutalism rolled up our overcast sky.

On this side of alienation, a river of disease plagued by
obscurity, recalcitrant as wisdom wounded the high buildings.

I can think I can think dialectically: addiction is the manifes-
tation of the commodity in human form. Recovery teaches life
beyond addiction & beyond acquiescence to sales traffic—

you know, the ethical life seems extreme to those not dis-
membered by a normal life. Now we can embrace negation
through abduction.

I explain how I held onto faith by threads between my navel
and backbone's cartilage contorted by your flexion that exerts
rigour, grit against the pressure of thoughtless thinking. I am
compelled to seek out difference because for so long I saw
someone else in the mirror.

The True recalibrates and reorients as I turn towards your
intrinsic essence; the world looks back at me through a cloud
of errors. It was poetry which actualised an ethics of distinction
for-itself outside commodified epithets about the secret life of
sentiments. You say to me *writing yourself out of addiction is so
brave*; I question your good intentions.

What concerns me is the physics of the meeting its chambers
full of a new sociality where community isn't made of astroturf.
I am at home in the quanta, absolute without notions of purity.
I sit with people as variegated as autumn in prayer our brows
press to the air's analemma: it's *all* Spirit;—

all that Spirit.

WOMBATS ARE NOT HOUSEHOLD PETS

> Nonsense is fugitive presence.
> —FRED MOTEN

The fruits of my recovery are fresh
with sterile seeds I spit them on
concrete steps they melt in the sun.

My gut is a worm eating my brain
the weather gets up so damn close
and I sow the grass with pollicitations.

I waited for you by the kissing gate
foraged for fresh sorrel tired of opening
my veins with a fan, trichotillomaniacal.

• • • •

At a poetry reading a white boy is on stage
telling us how the border and the empire
prevented him from going to a music festival.

I groan and generously overshare
brilliant facial contortions
there are no excuses to be quiet.

Old friends say don't think too much
about those things that make me mad
that way it would be easier to breathe.

She accidentally quotes a Tory proverb
clothes in every corner I look to lie down
at sunset when the sky just does *that*.

Everything is in motion.   We all tilt
at strange angles to the earth
nothing is firm in my hands anymore.

· · · ·

I tried to be calm in the public house
with pints of cordial, citrus and ice
listening for assonance and epiphany.

The rich never really worked a day
that is why I want to eat them all
you didn't understand my laughter.

Non-alcoholic beers for non-alcoholics
it escapes us as the tape plays forward.
I'd be drinking for eternity everlasting.

Queasy enough to retch a whole earth
my miraculous weapon against reason
now reduced to anxiety's dropped grin.

· · · ·

Azure light overcasts to downpour
the poetry wilts yesterday's orchids
I'm a serf amongst serifs in new
feudalism that burns close to home.

It was meant to be rock and roll
and I think, which is a terrible thing
oh no you've been thinking again
is this it? is this the dying world?

They are oblivious to my convulsions
just how beautiful I could be in ending.

      • • • •

When I stopped self-harming
they stopped inviting me out
I travel through the brickwork

surfing realism's highest road
I'm nonplussed, a closed circle,
no penguinization or autotheory
or cryptocurrency mysticism — ;

I'm unable to feel the Sunday breeze.
I am not that fazed by a boring death.

      • • • •

I had the desire to make art that could walk
out of a building onto a quiet suburban road
and be loud   enough to start.

The road's privatised and full of bunting;
it has no style.   I'm questioning
what community is if not forced togetherness.

Vladimir Mayakovsky fell in love
with his prison cell's keyhole —
I see through the same eyelet to ecology

in catastrophe. O I'm tired of being nuanced;
calls for resignations and general elections
don't provide me with hope in the Void.

The jungle came up through the carpet's
humid living room song of redemption
cloistered me in its riff to all day music.

Concomitantly, boomer generations love
to say we will all go from Marx and Engels
                    to Marks and Spencer.

But most of us are becoming more radical
with age we're unable to see out the breaks
we know wombats are not household pets.

[N A R C O P O E T I C S]

I am not a superhuman ball of lightning that is a mythic ideological construction of what cocaine is, the substance changes when the person taking it becomes a vessel for that substance.

Pop culture is full of lies.

I used to be chatty and really fun, these days I'm alone in a room, silent and full of odours.

Cocaine is nothing like height it's a falling; falling into a deep air hunger.

It may act as a stimulant for the first couple of casual experiments, it begins to induce the sensation of slowing down, right down until all you become is a bedsore falling all over yourself, with a sense of falling out of time, out of the world, and into a deep pit full of bluebottle flies.

The buzzing you hear is your own racing, which tells you: more; more; more.

Addiction is nothing like the books.

I'm not Sisyphus, but he is pushing a rock into my nose.

In this waking coma, paralysed nonchalance of paranoid sweating, thinking the creaks in the ceiling could be my mother's footsteps and, oh just maybe, I might be caught this time?

I probably won't, I'm far too good at directing the world around.

But the thought of having to pretend I'm asleep in the event of someone bursting through the door is electric, confident, and nauseous.

And now I embark on the cocaine odyssey by carefully cutting and scraping and sniffing.

I never question what goes into this strange hypnotic toxin.

I just believe in what's in it, putting it into me by any means necessary.

I lay the gear out into an X and push my nose through it.

Such naked duress.

Again.   Again.

. . .

Endurance can mean my capacity to endure drug use, to put my body through lines that, when totalled up, would go on for miles and miles.

I would often, when high, go out for a cigarette and end up smoking two or three in a row.

I imagined addiction as this never-ending cigarette.

A cigarette you couldn't stop smoking.

Addiction as endurance, then, impacts the very conception of time; a time that is lived without movement.

I was suspended in time, buoyant, jubilant, quickly floating with anhedonia, vomit, blood.

Denise Riley described the death of her son in *Time Lived, Without Its Flow*: 'You live inside a great circle with no rim'.[1]

I was living a line without end; a morning after that had no hope of reaching midday; enduring time in the duress of a continuous present; making the same choices hoping for a different outcome.

In medias relapse means I am relapsing.

A strange word that captures the immobilising thrill dovetailing with the shame and lack of self-care or even carelessness about the future.

Surely if I don't get away with this, the life I built for myself in the previous year of sobriety/abstinence/ Go(o)d, *surely* all of that is going up my nose.

Thoughts pass as bedsheet hallucinations in neon cuneiform.

It's raining outside.

---

1   Denise Riley, *Time Lived, Without Its Flow* (London: Capsule Editions, 2012), p.10.

The birds and the light coming in.

I'm blacking out and close to an overdose.

I'm in my grandmother's room.

She died here in 2013 of too much life, old age and myocarditis.

I'm on the edge here now, arrhythmia and vasoconstrictive palpitations.

But it isn't working anymore.

Sisyphus pushes more of the rocks up my nose.

I want more.

. . .

A study about dopamine and drugs at the University of Michigan by Kent Berridge and Terry Robinson discovered that drugs are addictive primarily because the huge increase of dopamine produced by them creates 'an artificial inflated intensity' which drives the phenomenon of craving. They label this 'incentive salience', a theory of addiction where the brain begins to react to overindulgence by deconstructing desire so that the addict is left wanting to do more without having the same results.[2]

It's territory for brain damage.

---

2   Maia Szalavitz, *Unbroken Brain* (New York: Picador, 2016), pp. 112-116.

Each line has the capacity to become 'a great experiential context', like Gregor Hens re-experiencing his first cigarette.[3] For Hens, reminiscing, remembering, recollecting, this first cigarette 'offered [him] an experience that was narratable for the very first time'.[4]

But the sad reality is, for alcoholics and addicts life passes in a blur.

It's not until you approach the hard rock at the bottom that you jolt back into the world and give yourself and your behaviour the context you need for it to become narratable.

That's the impetus behind the surrender; and I smash another line out.

• • •

The sense of time as without flow, is what Lisa Baraitser calls 'enduring time'.[5] It is a sense of living in a point of viscosity, stillness, unbecoming, formlessness, present-tense-ness: 'this caesura has duration. We differentially live it, are living in it, enduring it'.[6]

Addiction has duration and it is also caesurae in the individual's experience of temporal duration.

3   Gregor Hens, *Nicotine*, trans. Jen Calleja (London: Fitzcarraldo Editions, 2017), p.66.
4   Ibid., p. 67.
5   Lisa Baraitser, *Enduring Time* (London: Bloomsbury, 2017), p. 20.
6   Ibid., p. 7.

Relapse is the embrace of endurance.

It is a temporal experience without flow, with an excruciating duration.

There is nothing to suggest that a relapse is a single episode; there is nothing to prevent it becoming a way of life.

In Jeet Thayil's satirical rendering of the Bombay poets and artists of the 50s, *The Book of Chocolate Saints*, his narrator, Dismas Bambai—a heroin addict and journalist/poet—provides a telling answer: '[It's] [a] way of killing time. Time is stretched or compressed depending on how much you're holding and how much you've done. You're never bored, not until you quit, then all the time you killed comes back'.[7]

All that dead time rose in me like a zombified corpse of the person I used to know, the dead weight of that time just before sobriety, the dead labour of addiction.

• • •

Cocaine has prompted me to query the experience of enduring addiction, the endurance of addicts, temporal as well as psychophysiological.

Only the letters on the page, the stillness of words against great white indistinction, may provide a way out.

---

7   Jeet Thayil, *The Book of Chocolate Saints* (London: Faber and Faber, 2018) p.109.

I am writing to recover; I am writing to stay alive.

I was a member of society, I was sober, I was happy to tell every-one what I was recovering from.

And then I wasn't.

Recovery contained for me, and still does even as a possibility, a sense of what Sianne Ngai calls 'stuplimity': a sense of 'over-whelming excitement and stultifying boredom emanating from the same object'.[8]

That object is, more accurately, an experience of time.

I found recovery stuplimitous, should such a word begin to sig-nify.

I lacked perspective on what I'd managed to achieve.

A year had passed and I was in the best shape of my life, but I was rapidly falling, lapsing, blurring, enduring my own ingrat-itude, walking a long road into lines of discontent, restlessness, and irritability.

Nothing was, is, or will ever be enough.

I had yet to let go of the ravenous craving for more; more; more.

Where I used to greet the day with thoughts of affirmation and compassion, my mind started running on autopilot.

---

8   Qtd in Baraitser, *Enduring Time*, p. 17.

I was meant to feel spiritually awakened, free, responsible, but all of this ended up compounding my already-existing feelings of containment, restriction, asynchronicity with other peoples' time.

I would walk into the rooms of 12 step meetings with an 'I'm doing sweet, mate' veneer, a smile that was so white it told the story of what would come next, a crook between the left corner of my lips and cheek, not quite sinister, but sick.

. . .

'Incentive salience' means wanting something but not liking it. It means desire escalates but pleasure doesn't.

My lip quivers.

The weird colours that penetrate me when I close my eyes form the faces of my mother and partner and their tears, when I eventually get honest with them.

I'll do it tomorrow.

They will berate me or be disappointed and I'll know I shouldn't be in this state but all I think about is the next line, the next sip of water because I've heard you process the bump through your kidneys and so if you want to lessen chances of death you should flush it out as soon as you put it in.

Incentive salience in medias relapse is a pathological overlearning of the process of insufflation.

When will I put the straw down and stop inhaling?

What kind of breathing is it?

. . .

There's a rattle in my chest.

Sisyphus has made it so far into my sinus that the rocks are trickling down my throat.

I'm doing so much packet I'm post-nasal, poststructuralist, post-colonial, post-ideological but definitely not post/past cocaine.

White noise, the sound of sniffing, the rumble of tolerance.

I decide to crush up Valium into the snow on my bedside table and drink a bottle of camomile tincture and then a bottle of homeopathic drops that help with nausea and then I wait.

I'm begging myself to sleep, my heart to calm down and to be able to breathe through my nose again.

. . .

The long lie-ins have started again going to sleep exhausted and waking up as if my duvet was covered in weight plates with an alarm clock whinging at me like Shia LaBeouf quacking into camera one: just do it.

I was a year sober.

And then I felt the click of a switch, a series of synapses blowing neural dust off themselves, as if a box had been ticked, as if suddenly I had decided or arrived at the decision that I was fixed, I was normal, I could enjoy the night, yes, the night, no longer keeping it in the day, just keeping it in the evening, like everyone else who wasn't an addict.

I was about to experience life after sunset; I wanted to become the night; I was becoming the night.

I hosted a poetry reading for my fledgling small press with unsure footing, leaning on the bar to ease myself into a 'normal' pint, none of that 0% or 0.5% shit, the normal stuff, for normal people, like me, being normal, doing normal things, leaning at the bar, drinking normally.

And then another and another and another until I was spinning.

. . .

Being drunk is feeling time move all around you but you, yourself, are still; a rock, an anchor; yes, I was grounded now, I felt my feet, felt them call my backside into a chair, felt my palms cradle my head, felt the warm embrace; and I endured; I persevered; and then the thought of getting cocaine was on me.

There must have been something else other than alcohol in the beer; there must be something else in alcohol other than alcohol.

It was as if a seed had been swallowed with the first, sowed with the rest, and then it was germinating; flowering; quickening into an obsession.

I felt liberated by this obsession, fixation, absolute seizure by compulsion.

I thought myself steadfast, strong, obstinate, refusing to give up being myself, my true self, beneath all the water, a layer of stone, something concrete in me rising up through all the repression, suppression, digression, a huge slab of me, undying, unbecoming and then becoming true, regurgitating a desire, a drive, a monumental weight of discovery as if for the first time I was feeling this sensation to score.

I began sniffing in air, anticipation made me clam up, more light entered my peripherals, back straightened, I talked with more confidence, persuaded reluctant students to buy books, I sold other peoples' books with the same enthusiasm and passion I usually saved for the ones I published.

I greeted everyone with a huge embrace, eagerly wanting their love and craving their attention.

· · ·

The search for the subject of addiction is, contrary to Avital Ronell's assertion that 'Being-on-drugs' has 'everything to do with the bad conscience of our era', actually the a priori state of being-wanting-drugs.[9]

---

9   Avital Ronell, *Crack Wars* (Chicago: University of Illinois Press, 2004), p.3.

Being-on-drugs always already implies the drop, the score, the exchange; it is a state of fractured interiority that requires the precession, the lapse into consumption of an illicit substance.

Whilst Ronell is correct in underscoring that 'drugs are *libidinally invested*' what such investment necessitates as a precondition or proviso is the libidinal condition of want, need, desire pure and simple, a motivation to invest in the first instance.[10]

I was assured, quivering with a bristled, dangerous excitement on the shore between history and ontology.

It was Nietzschean, this trembling, calling into question the very history of narcotics as he did in *The Gay Science*, wondering what links 'high-culture' with '*high*-culture', and I was asking people to consume-purchase-buy-sit-drink.

I had spent so long living vicariously through them, this crowd of dear friends and associates, watching their breath turn to smatterings of ale-stained stupefaction, and now within myself I felt that surge into being, desire unchained, boundless and ready.

This is precisely what Burroughs meant when he wrote about the 'algebra of need'; it is a strange equation of oneself with others through the substance, through the very decision to ingest a substance, as if filling oneself up with the substance gave one substance of an altogether different quality.

Substance abuse qualifies the relationship between '*fractal interiorities*' or states of 'immanence' in which endurance is tested on the basis of its rooting out of connection.[11]

10 Ibid., p.25.
11 Ibid., p.15.

• • •

It's not petrichor; it's just the strange chemical sweat I'm exuding; it's not rain; it's just coke water on my forehead.

I brush it away, I want to push the water out of my eyes and then they swell up and my nose is bleeding.

The other varieties (cutting agents) start doing labour.

I have capacity again and my heart is returning to normal.

I check the clock on my phone, it's 6am.

I started at 8pm the evening before.

How has all this time elapsed?

How did I end up lying here relapsing, sweating, moving lower and lower in search of dopaminergic wakefulness?

Sisyphus starts at the bottom again, slugging the rock up my nose and I return to worse.

The last thought I have before I fall asleep is: what if my gear is contaminated with coronavirus?

And then a little white rock trickled out of my tear duct.

I manage to scoop it off my cheek and rub it into my gums.

But I can't sleep.

I want to know what is in this stuff; if the drugs stop working then there can't be enough drugs in the drugs.

What is going on?

I check my phone, licking the screen to see if there is any gear left on it.

I type in what the fuck is going on with cocaine in the UK to Google.

This country is obsessed with white power/powder!

In the last five years, cocaine use has doubled in the UK.[12]

Purity is at a record high.[13]

The world market for cocaine in 2006 was worth an estimated $400 billion.

There are traces of it on 5% of all UK banknotes.[14]

Wastewater analysis shows that 1 in 50 people use it every day in London.[15]

In May 2019, King's College London and the University of Suffolk collaborated and found that 100% of fresh water shrimp tested positive for traces of cocaine.

---

12 Abby Young-Powell, 'Cocaine use doubles in Britain in five years...', *Independent* (May 2019).

13 Ibid.

14 Ibid.

15 Ibid.

Imagine that.

Wired and absolutely fucking mad shrimp.

At the University of Naples Federico II, they've looked into how cocaine traces are fucking with eels.[16]

Yes, eels!

The eels are high and under duress.

Like the shrimp.

Cocaine is in the water.

There is something in the water.

They even make rehabs for eels now, giving them clean water for 10 days to prevent muscle damage and lower their cortisol levels.[17]

Those poor shrimp can't go to rehab; a rehab doesn't exist for shrimp.

And I sit there off my face at the ridiculousness of these statistics and facts.

Who in their right mind would contribute to this kind of bio-and-eco-politics?

---

16   Frances Perraudin, 'Purity of cocaine in Europe at highest level in decade…', *Guardian* (June 2018).

17   Ibid.

I want to know right now what the statistic is for people who can peel a satsuma without it breaking.

That is a statistic worth fighting for, I think, as I lay out another line and inhale.

The eels and the shrimp look back at me on the black mirror.

ACKNOWLEDGEMENTS

With gratitude to everyone doing 12 step fellowship work, my sponsors past and present, fellows, and everyone in search of sobriety; to Zenobia, Anand, and Gyan Sharma, Auntie Coco, Tariq and Yusuf, and all my extended family for giving me strength and encouragement in my most vulnerable moments; to Sarona Abuaker for teaching me love, freedom and joy; to Mo and Suzie for their compassion; to Kashif, Anu, Bhanu, Sopo, Aisheshek, Ash, Dhanveer, Keston, Joe L, Joe M, Ed, Danny, Cole, Dom, Rob, Sean, Sabeen, Nilu, Luke R, Luke W, Luke M, Marissa, Oscar, Verity, John W, Peter, Jessie, Aaron, Stuart, Rana, Nada, Emma, Anthony V., Sophie, Daniella, Kat A, Shani, Danah, Reem, Alia, for your friendship, inspiration, and kindness during the difficult days; to Stephen and Lara Sheehi and to Janey Starling for teaching me that the revolution will be sober; to everyone not mentioned here that I've met through poetry—I love you; to Sara Crangle for teaching me Modernism as an undergraduate and changing how my brain worked; to Katherine Angel for helping me find confidence in my writing at a critical moment during the Covid 19 pandemic; to Lewis R. Gordon, Paget Henry, Jane Anna Gordon, Jackie Martinez, Vialcary Crisóstomo, Devonya Havis, Michael Monohan, Greg Doukas, and everyone else I've met and will meet through the Caribbean Philosophical Association—I have never felt more connected and free of addiction than in your company; to Stephen Motika and Anthony Anaxagorou for their sage editorial advice; to my agent Suresh for his patience and wisdom; to my therapist M., psychiatrist Dr. Az, and my acupuncturist Myles for keeping me alive; to the editors of Dodo Ink's *Trauma* anthology for publishing an earlier unfinished version of 'Narcopoetics' in 2021; and to you, dear reader, for supporting this book.

The epigraphs are borrowed with gratitude from:

Ghalib, Mirza Asadullah Khan, Ghalib: *Selected Poems and Letters*, trans. Frances W. Pritchett and Owen T. A. Cornwall (New York: Columbia University Press, 2017)

Beckett, Samuel, *Molloy* (London: Faber & Faber, 2009)

Glissant, Èdouard, *Poetic Intention*, trans. Nathanaël (New York: Nightboat Books, 2010)

Moten, Fred, *Stolen Life* (Durham: Duke University Press, 2018)

A Z A D   A S H I M   S H A R M A is the director of the87press and the author of *Against the Frame* (originally published by Barque Press in 2017 with a 5th Anniversary edition released by Broken Sleep Books in 2022) and *Ergastulum: Vignettes of Lost Time* (Broken Sleep Books 2022). He was awarded The Nicolás Cristóbal Guillén Batista Outstanding Book Award 2023 by the Caribbean Philosophical Association. He is currently a PhD Candidate in English and Humanities at Birkbeck College. His poetry and essays have been published widely and internationally, most recently in *Wasafiri*.

NIGHTBOAT BOOKS

Nightboat Books, a nonprofit organization, seeks to develop audiences for writers whose work resists convention and transcends boundaries. We publish books rich with poignancy, intelligence, and risk. Please visit nightboat.org to learn about our titles and how you can support our future publications.

The following individuals have supported the publication of this book. We thank them for their generosity and commitment to the mission of Nightboat Books:

Kazim Ali • Anonymous (8) • Mary Armantrout • Jean C. Ballantyne • Thomas Ballantyne • Bill Bruns • John Cappetta • V. Shannon Clyne • Ulla Dydo Charitable Fund • Photios Giovanis • Amanda Greenberger • Vandana Khanna • Isaac Klausner • Shari Leinwand • Anne Marie Macari • Elizabeth Madans • Martha Melvoin • Caren Motika • Elizabeth Motika • The Leslie Scalapino - O Books Fund • Robin Shanus • Thomas Shardlow • Rebecca Shea • Ira Silverberg • Benjamin Taylor • David Wall • Jerrie Whitfield & Richard Motika • Arden Wohl • Issam Zineh

This book is made possible, in part, by grants from the New York City Department of Cultural Affairs in partnership with the City Council, the New York State Council on the Arts Literature Program, and the National Endowment for the Arts.

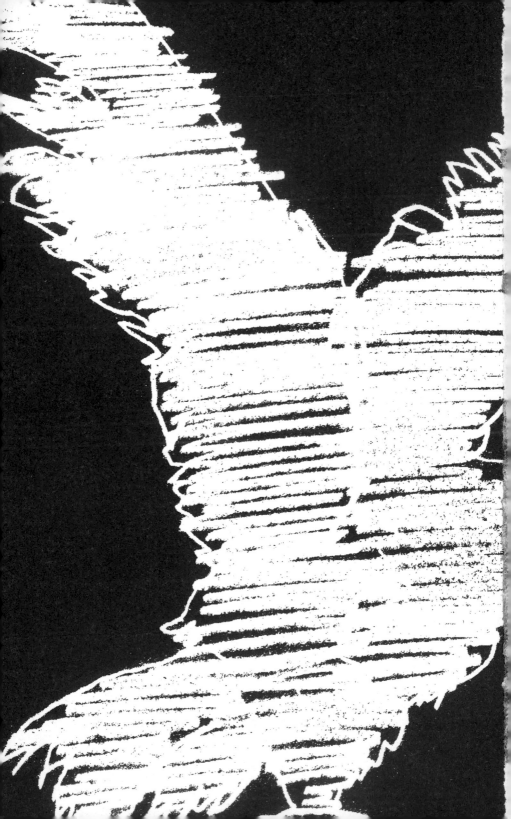